RUN! JUMP! PLAY!

HEALTHY ACTIVE HABITS

Mary Elizabeth Salzmann

Consulting Editor,
Diane Craig, M.A./ Reading Specialist

Sandcastle

An Imprint of Abdo Publishing
www.abdopublishing.com

www.abdopublishing.com

Published by Abdo Publishing, a division of ABDO, PO Box 398166, Minneapolis, Minnesota 55439. Copyright © 2015 by Abdo Consulting Group, Inc. International copyrights reserved in all countries. No part of this book may be reproduced in any form without written permission from the publisher. SandCastle™ is a trademark and logo of Abdo Publishing.

Printed in the United States of America, North Mankato, Minnesota
102014
012015

THIS BOOK CONTAINS
RECYCLED MATERIALS

Editor: Alex Kuskowski
Content Developer: Nancy Tuminelly
Cover and Interior Design: Colleen Dolphin, Mighty Media, Inc.
Photo Credits: Shutterstock

SandCastle™ Level: Transitional

SandCastle™ books are created by a team of professional educators, reading specialists, and content developers around five essential components—phonemic awareness, phonics, vocabulary, text comprehension, and fluency—to assist young readers as they develop reading skills and strategies and increase their general knowledge. All books are written, reviewed, and leveled for guided reading, early reading intervention, and Accelerated Reader® programs for use in shared, guided, and independent reading and writing activities to support a balanced approach to literacy instruction. The SandCastle™ series has four levels that correspond to early literacy development. The levels are provided to help teachers and parents select appropriate books for young readers.

EMERGING · BEGINNING · **TRANSITIONAL** · FLUENT

CONTENTS

WHAT IS A HEALTHY HABIT?

Being **active** is a healthy **habit**.

Being **active** helps your **muscles** grow strong.

Being **active** helps you feel good.

It's important to be **active** every day.

11

Kelly takes her dog to the dog park. They run together.

13

Seth plays soccer after school.

15

Alana and Maya ride bikes in the park.

18

Hunter goes **sledding** in the winter.

Courtney is on a softball team. She plays left field.

21

What is your **favorite** way to be **active**?

HEALTH QUIZ

1. Being **active** does not help you feel good. True or False?

2. Seth plays soccer after school. True or False?

3. Alana and Maya ride bikes in the park. True or False?

4. Hunter goes snowboarding in the winter. True or False?

5. Courtney plays first base. True or False?

Answers: 1. False 2. True 3. True 4. False 5. False

GLOSSARY

active – moving around or doing something.

favorite – someone or something that you like best.

habit – a behavior done so often that it becomes automatic.

muscle – the tissue connected to the bones that allows body parts to move.

sledding – the act of riding down a snowy hill on a sled, disk, or inner tube.